Wings of Desire—Angels of Berlin
Lothar Heinke

Wings of Desire—Angels of Berlin
Original hardcover December 2012
New edition 2024

Text: Lothar Heinke
Pictures and Cover Design: Eva C. Schweitzer
Picture p. 4: Mike Wolff
Picture p. 17: Landesarchiv Berlin
Picture p. 70: Funkturmverlag
Picture p. 78: Public domain
All other pictures: © Eva C. Schweitzer
Translation: Cindy Opitz
Copy editing: Franca Wolf

Printed in the United States and the EU
ISBN: 978-3-96026-092-9
Haradcover: 978-1-935902-14-0, 978-1-935902-19-5

© Berlinica Publishing LLC
165 West 83rd St., Suite 51, New York, NY, 10024, USA
https://berlinica.com

All rights reserved under International and Pan-American Copyright Law. No part of this book may be used or reproduced in any manner whatsoever without written permission except in the case of brief quotations embodied in critical articles and reviews.

Wings of Desire

Angels of Berlin

Lothar Heinke

Berlin and New York, 2012

LOTHAR HEINKE, a Berlin native, worked as a senior reporter for the East Berlin paper Der Morgen (The Morning) until 1991. After the Wall fell, he joined Tagesspiegel, Berlin's leading daily. He wrote about the transformation of Checkpoint Charlie and changes in the former GDR, and he also penned Berlin metro stories. In 2005, he published the book Fernsehturm Berlin (The Berlin TV Tower). Though retired now, he continues to work for Tagesspiegel. He lives with his wife in Berlin-Mitte, likes to listen to music (especially classical), loves traveling in Italy, and is a member of the Berlin 1FC Union soccer club.

Foto: Mike Wolff

EVA C. SCHWEITZER is the founder of Berlinica Publishing LLC, a book author and journalist with twenty-five years of experience. Originally a metro reporter in Berlin, she has spent most of the last fifteen years writing about the United States, including a Ph.D. about the Disneyfication of Times Square and the story collection Manhattan Moments.

BERLINICA PUBLISHING LLC is a New York-based multi-media publisher about Berlin, offering fiction, non-fiction, travel guides, history books, cookbooks, movies on DVD, music CDs, and wall calendars. All titles are in English or subtitled.

Get your own angel on a T-shirt, mug, necklace, or iPad case at:
www.zazzle.com/Berlinica und www.cafepress.com/Berlinica.

Berlin's Guardian Angels

THE LARGE golden angel that stands guard over Berlin is too big to miss and can be seen from every direction. She is the goddess Victoria, and her wings are dazzling in the sun's rays. Those who brave the 285 steps to the platform beneath her enjoy a spectacular angel's-eye view of the city. Berlin locals commonly refer to their most famous lady as "Golden Else." Filmmaker Wim Wenders perched a guardian angel on her shoulders, high above Berlin, and Barack Obama once spoke at her feet.

Berlin is home to many more angels: heavenly angels in places of worship, guardian angels watching over building doors and outdoor markets, decorative angels in ice cream parlors, pizzerias, and museums, Prussian angels celebrating victory over Napoleon, and angels offering comfort in cemeteries. The Berlin actress known around the world as the "Blue Angel"—Marlene Dietrich—was laid to rest in the cemetery on Stubenrauchstrasse. Christian Daniel Rauch, who created the angel of peace above Mehringplatz in the district of Kreuzberg, lies in the Dorotheenstadt Cemetery. Berlin's angel of theater, Bertold Brecht, is also buried there, and his Berliner Ensemble is adorned with cheerful cherubs, too. Through all of the twists and turns of Berlin's history, these heavenly messengers have imparted aid, affluence, and an enduring sense of vitality.

Berlin, already a thriving metropolis with over a million inhabitants by the end of the nineteenth century, has certainly had its share of guardian angels. They didn't necessarily have wings or speak like you and I, but they definitely watched over those who found their fortunes in the Gründerzeit and throughout the prosperous Golden Twenties. They are not easily tamed, however, and seemed to disappear for a while, when the city seemed lost to the devil and the country cowered under a rain of firebombs. Classical angels, from the Brandenburg Gate to the City Palace, went up in flames, and countless angels in Berlin churches joined the human casualties. After the war, bombs, and blokkade, the city was torn in two. Eastern Germany put up barbed wire and walls, right through St. Hedwig's Cemetery and the Invalidenfriedhof (Veterans Cemetery), whose angels lay broken on the ground. Families were divided, friends kept apart. And the Berlin City Palace was destroyed, along with its angel; only a single pair survived, on the Eosanderportal.

Guardian angels were urgently needed in both sides of the city. One, John F. Kennedy, gave Berliners hope when he stood before hundreds of thousands of people and said that everyone in the world who fights for peace can say, "Ich bin ein Berliner!" Later, Ronald Reagan called on Soviet Party Chief Gorbachev to "tear down this Wall!" On November 9, 1989, the angels arranged a miracle: the Wall fell. Then the guardian angels helped Berlin to rise again, as East and West grew together once more. Many angels were restored: Victoria atop the Brandenburg Gate, the angels along the Schlossbrücke (Palace Bridge), on the Zeughaus (Armory), and the Neue Wache (New Guardhouse). This new, single, and sometimes united Berlin calls out, "Thank you, Angels. The city needs you like Berliners need air to breathe."

Lothar Heinke

Prussian Angels

Victoria and Napoleon

Prussian Angels adorn the imperial boulevard Unter den Linden, from the Brandenburg Gate to the Schlossplatz (Palace Square). They herald Prussia's victory over Napoleon, mourn fallen warriors, or stand guard over royal gates. Many represent Greek and Roman goddesses, in bronze or marble, like Victoria in the quadriga on the Brandenburg Gate, the city's symbol built by Carl Gotthard Langhans around 1790, modeled after the Propylaia on the Acropolis in Athens. Napoleon captured the quadriga and sent it back to Paris as war loot, but it was returned after Napoleon's defeat. Since then, Victoria holds an Iron Cross and the Prussian Eagle. The Brandenburg Gate was off limits while Berlin remained divided, but in 1989, Berliners stood on top of the Wall and later demanded its removal. Today the Brandenburg Gate is a symbol of German unity.

The Schlossbrucke (Palace Bridge) spans the Kupfergraben Canal at the east end of Unter den Linden, built by Karl Friedrich Schinkel in the early 1820s. Figures carved in carrara marble stand on granite bases, many with wings, representing Greek goddesses.

Winged Companions to Fallen Warriors

THE MARBLE angels on the Schlossbrücke depict the life and suffering of a warrior, led by the greek goddess Nike, who carries the fallen hero to Olympus.

Risen Angels Appeal for Peace

ANGELS LINGER above the columns of the Neue Wache (New Guardhouse) on Unter den Linden, ready to accompany fallen soldiers to heaven (opposite page). This building was created by Karl Friedrich Schinkel in 1818 and the winged goddess of victory by Johann Gottfried Schadow. During the German Democratic Republic's rule after World War II, the Neue Wache was deemed a "monument to the victims of fascism and militarism."

Today it is the central memorial of the Federal Republic. There's a large Pieta inside by Käthe Kollwitz—a mother mourning her dead son, representing a protest against war.

The entrance to the Staatsrat (State Council) building is graced by two angels (below). It was originally part of the City Palace that was severely damaged by bombs during World War II and torn down by the GDR. Only this portal remained. It was from here that the Socialist leader Karl Liebknecht proclaimed the Free Socialist Republic after the revolution of 1918.

War-wounded Angels in the Old Armory

THIS WINGED Victoria (opposite page) stands in the foyer of the most beautiful Baroque building in Berlin, the former Armory, completed in 1706, which houses the Deutsches Historisches Museum (German History Museum). The larger-than-life goddess greets visitors in the entrance hall, the former Hall of Fame of the Prussian Army's. Now she illustrates greatness and weakness alike, as her right arm and left hand were victims of World War II. Many figures decorate the Armory, including divine heralds and cherubs (left).

Winged Muses on Wild Animals

THE GENDARMENMARKT is the most beautiful square in Berlin and home to the Konzerthaus (Concert Hall). It was originally the royal theater, built from 1818 to 1821 by Karl Friedrich Schinkel, and is flanked by the German and French Cathedrals. Reduced to a heap of rubble during World War II, the square was restored in the 1970s. Today, lions and panthers stand guard on the stairs, and muses with instruments invite visitors to enjoy a festive musical experience. As the poet Thomas Carlyle once said, "Music is well said to be the speech of angels."

Peace Column — Warrior Angel

THE ANGEL on Zietenplatz (below), formerly Wilhelmplatz along the government mile on Wilhelmstrasse, has a military bent: he guards the bronze monument of Army General Leopold von Dessau, who fought in the 1745 Battle of Kesselsdorf, when Frederick the Great defeated Saxony and Austria. There were no guardian angels, however, for the 20,000 dead and wounded sacrificed on the battlefield. The Peace Column (left) is less militaristic. It stands in the middle of Kreuzberg's Belle-Alliance-Platz since 1843, an open space on the southern end of Friedrichstrasse called Mehringplatz today. The Victoria atop the column, by Christian Daniel Rauch, also symbolizes Prussia's victory over France.

Paris, Kreuzberg: The Green Angel

The National monument in the "in" district of Kreuzberg is a tall Gothic spire created by famed architect Karl Friedrich Schinkel. The angels that adorn it (opposite page), cast in 1821, commemorate the Prussian wars of independence. The tower is crowned by an Iron Cross, awarded to Friedrich Wilhelm III for exceptional service during the battle for national independence. The cast-iron tower stands over 62 feet tall and crowns the Kreuzberg, the highest point in Berlin and the city's only mountain with a waterfall (albeit an artificial one).

The monument affords an expansive view of the Kreuzberg, Mitte, and Tiergarten districts and is a popular spot for a picnic—like the one in the photo below.

PARIS
den 30 Mnrz
1814

Party Angels

Patroness Victoria

GOLDEN ELSE is the city's guardian angel, spreading her wings high above the Tiergarten and looking westward to Charlottenburg. Mark Twain thought she looked strange from behind. In the movie *Wings of Desire*, Wim Wenders sat his angels on her shoulder to reflect. "Perhaps I longed for these creatures to exist, so they could increase our chances of survival through the power of good thoughts," he once said.

Victoria, who also commemorates Prussia's victory over France, Austria, and Denmark, is a heavy hunk of metal: 27 feet tall, 35 tons, and decked in two and a half pounds of gold leaf; the column alone on which she stand measures over 164 feet tall. She towers over a traffic island, and an observation platform affords a view up her billowing skirt.

Victoria is never lonely, but once a year, in June, she's surrounded by bright cars, colorful demonstrators, and loud music. The annual Christopher Street Day Parade winds through the Tiergarten and past the golden angel, when Berlin's happiest angels celebrate all day long.

Heaven Can Wait

"LEARN TO dance, otherwise the angels in heaven won't know what to do with you," St. Augustine once said. These not-so-heavenly angels at Nollendorfplatz, at the Christopher Street Day Parade don't need to be told twice. And in Berlin, as the Prussian king Frederick the Great was known to say, everyone should be happy in his own fashion.

Life is a Cabaret: Remembering Sally Bowles

Nollendorfplatz has been an amusement mecca since the Roaring Twenties, when Christopher Isherwood wrote *Berlin Stories*, about the fictional actress and singer Sally Bowles—the novel on which the musical *Cabaret* was based. A plaque at 17 Nollendorfstraße marks the apartment of the author. Left: An „angel" at the parade.

Angels on Wheels: Roll out the Barrel!

What do Berlin angels do when they're thirsty? They rent a beer bike—a bar on wheels, with beer on tap. Only in Berlin! City code limits consumption to ten pints per hour (or so these happy folks claim), which is definitely enough to annoy Berlin bus drivers and everybody else. As the song says, "Roll out the barrel, and we'll have a barrel of fun!" Best to be on the safe side, though, with your very own guardian angel to go, like the ones below, from KaDeWe, Berlin's biggest department store at Wittenbergplatz.

The Blue Angel—Curry under the Elevated Train

The Blue Angel was no heavenly creature, but a (fictional) seedy dockside cabaret in a small German town, where sensual singer Lola befuddled poor Professor Immanuel Rath—to the point that his students called him "Professor Unrat" (Professor Garbage), the German title of Heinrich Mann's novel. The *Blue Angel* arrived on the silver screen in 1930 and catapulted Marlene Dietrich to international fame with the song *Falling in Love Again*. The Marlene on the opposite page adorns the elevated train pylons of Metro Line 2 in Berlin's Prenzlauer Berg district, where Konnopke pedals Currywurst, a Berlin institution. Max Konnopke established the snack bar in 1930, which is owned by his daughter, Waltraud Ziervogel, today. Across from her shop is the fancier Filetstück restaurant, where your wallet might need a guardian angel.

Twin Angels

Cherubs in Pairs

ARE ANGELS like snowflakes, each one unique? Given the plethora of twin angels around town, you might wonder whether the artists who created them thought they might bring double the luck or blessings to the homes and churches they adorned. Or did the people who commissioned them just have more money? These little angels say a lot without saying a word. Many are *putti*, an Italian word for "little boys," and some are more like messengers of Eros, god of love, than guardians. But what difference does it make? According to poet Terri Guillemets, angels subscribe to only one philosophy: Love.

Kreuzberg Miniatures

These cherubs (opposite page), guard an administrative building in Kreuzberg's Lindenstrasse, originally built for the Victoria Insurance Company. Below, a pair of angels on Friedrichstrasse holds Berlin's coat of arms, a bear with a crown. The angels above adorn the Martin-Gropius-Bau, an art museum built in the Italian Renaissance style by Martin Gropius, great uncle of Walter Gropius (the architect who founded the Bauhaus School).

Church Cherubs, Monastery Twins

TWIN ANGELS can be found in many Berlin churches, like the ones on this page from the Parochial Church, or the ones on the facing page from St. Mary's (above), and St. Nicholas (below). They often crown altar pieces or remind us of the finite nature of life, like the ones below.

Church Angels

Zwinglikirche, Cultural Center, Friedrichshain

WHY IS IT called the "Zwinglikirche Cultural Center"? Though established as a place of worship in 1908, it no longer served in a religious capacity after the Wall was built in 1961. The grand building seemed to be asleep. After the Wall fell, residents around Osthafen and the Oberbaumbrücke (Oberbaum Bridge), fueled by a great deal of passion and enthusiasm, ended the Sleeping Beauty's slumber.

Since 2007, the Zwinglikirche Cultural Organization has restored the historical monument's purpose. The old church has become a meeting place once again, host to exhibitions, political discussions, films, and readings. And the angel bearing the baptismal font (opposite page), like so many in Berlin churches, stands watch over the cultural center's visitors, still promoting wisdom, beauty, and justice.

Guardian at The Wall: St. Michael in Kreuzberg

The Guardian at the Engelbecken (Angel's Pool): Archangel Michael, the pool's namesake and conqueror over Satan, stands guard where the Wall used to be. St. Michael's was built as a garrison church in the 1850s by August Soller, a student of Karl Friedrich Schinkel. The church soon became the Catholic community church of the rapidly expanding Luisenstadt district. Poet Theodor Fontane once described it as the most beautiful church in Berlin. It was destroyed during World War II, and the steeple was restored in the 1960s. The church's white marble angel (opposite page) is nearly 33 feet tall and was originally created by sculptor August Kiss; a copy crowns the steeple today. Below: Mosaics embellish the church's doors, depicting Maria and Archangel Gabriel.

The Heart of Berlin: Mitte's St. Nicholas

BERLIN'S OLDEST house of worship (pictured left) is located in the Nikolai quarter, where Berlin began and the very first Berliners lived and worked—over 800 years ago. Shortly after the Reformation, pastor and composer Paul Gerhardt preached here. The church was destroyed in World War II, and was rebuilt in the 1980s, when its double steeple was also restored. Today the house of worship is an exhibition hall for the City Museum for Protestant History in Berlin. And the many angels floating in the altar room (below and opposite), hanging by nearly invisible lines (albeit without the altars they used to adorn), still greet us today from the distant Middle Ages.

Gothic and Gold
St. Mary's in Mitte

St. Mary's Church, the second oldest parish church in Berlin, located between the Fernsehturm (TV Tower) and Alexanderplatz, was first documented in 1292. It was the original Berliners' church, in what was then Neustadt (New City) between Alexanderplatz and the Spree River. St. Mary's consists of a three-aisled nave with tall Gothic windows. The brick construc-

tion stands on a cobblestone base. Inside, sarcophagi and tomb slabs of rich mediaeval citizens are displayed, along with a fresco from 1485, *The Dance of Death*. Occasional organ concerts are held in this Protestant church, in which Martin Luther King Jr. once preached at the invitation of the German Democratic Republic. Even the organ is surrounded by golden angels.

Huguenots and Poles: Hedwig's Cathedral

FREDERICK THE Great commissioned Berlin's main Catholic church in 1773: Hedwig's Cathedral at Opernplatz, today Bebelplatz. Georg Wenzeslaus von Knobelsdorff and Jean Laurent Le Geay designed the church with its angel frescoes and green cupola after the Pantheon in Rome. The church is named for St. Hedwig, Duchess of Silesia around 1200, who is said to have gone barefoot in winter out of pity for the poor. The church was destroyed in 1943 and rebuilt ten years later. Since the Wall fell, tens of thousands of Catholic Poles have immigrated to Berlin again.

Stronghold of God: The Berlin Cathedral

NOT ONLY is the façade of the Berlin Cathedral full of winged statues, but the interior of the city's largest Protestant church, built in 1905, is full of grandiose splendor as well. Prussian emperors and kings were baptized and wed in the cathedral, many of which found their final resting place in the crypt beneath it. Today, the tombs and ornamented sarcophagi from the 15th through the 19th centuries are open to the public. Devotions, worship services, and organ and choir concerts take place in the cathedral, which is also where Hugo von Hofmannsthal's play *Jedermann* (Everyman) found a stage, about the life and death of a rich man.

Classical Masterpiece: Friedrichswerder Church

ARCHANGEL MICHAEL stands guard here, too, above the main entrance of the former Friedrichswerder Church (opposite page). Built by the architect and sculptor Karl Friedrich Schinkel from 1824 to 1830, the church lies along the Kupfergraben, an arm of the Spree River, where Berlin was established in 1237. The angel was originally made of terracotta, but when war damage was repaired in the 1980s, a new bronze angel replaced the original. More than a dozen smaller angels adorn the bronze church door (left). Today, the church is a museum for Schinkel; it contains many of his works of art, surrounded by glowing glass windows depicting angels bound for heaven (above left).

Mortal Angels: Museum of the Mark

The Berlin and Mark Brandenburg Heritage Museum looks like a small castle. Its red brick tower is visible from far away, rising up from the Spree River, on whose banks the Märkisches Museum was built in 1902. Architect Ludwig Hoffmann copied buildings from all over the Brandenburg Mark, from the castle keep of the Old Bishops Castle in Wittstock, to the city of Brandenburg's Katharinenkirche, the Town Hall in Tangermünde, and the Brandenburg Roland, a monument made of Middle Triassic muschelkalk in 1474. The figurine shown at the opposite page is a wooden church angels carefully restored by the museum.

Tomb Angels

Harbingers of Heaven

There are hundreds of angels to be found on gravestones in Berlin cemeteries, where they offer comfort and point the way toward heaven when the time has come for the rich and poor, famous and unknown alike, though the biggest, most beautiful marble angels are more likely to be found with the rich and famous.

Invalidenfriedhof, final resting place for the Prussian military, was established on Scharnhorststrasse in the mid-18th century. Among the generals buried here are Field Marshal Hermann Ludwig Leopold Gottlieb von Boyen, whose grave (right) is adorned by two nearly identical angels, designed by August Stüler. While Berlin was divided, Invalidenfriedhof was on the line between East and West. When the Wall was built, the cemetery became part of the heavily guarded forbidden zone of the border installation. Thousands of graves were destroyed—first by the war, and then by the Wall; of 3000 graves, only a few hundred remain. After World War II, the four victorious Allies originally intended to level the cemetery completely, to wipe Prussia from people's memories, but never followed through with the plan.

Veterans Cemetery: Prussians in Beijing

THE JUGENDSTIL angel (opposite), made from white marble, adorns the grave of Director General Eduard Julius Nolte. Below left: Angel at the tomb of Prussian War Minister Job von Witzleben, designed by Prussian master builder Karl Friedrich Schinkel.

Below right: Gravestone angel of Major General Karl Julius von Gross, also known as Schwarzhoff, who fought in the Boxer Rebellion in China. He died—like a true Prussian—trying to rescue documents during a fire at the imperial palace in Beijing.

St. Hedwig's Cemetery: Angels behind Barbed Wire

This Doesn't happen every day: a sculptor designs praying angels whose upswept wings flank the entrance to a cemetery where he himself will someday find his final resting place. Josef Limburg, born in 1874, embellished the city's oldest Catholic cemetery with his creation and was later buried there. St. Hedwig's and two other burial grounds are located near Chausseestrasse, and was also part of the border installation and death strip between the Wall and Hinterland Wall that divided Berlin for almost three decades. Most of the graves were leveled by GDR border troops, and Limburg's angels were trapped behind barbed wire. Today the Wall is gone, save a small piece preserved as a historic monument, but the green grass tells us what was once here. Only the angels at the entrance are silent.

Dorotheenstadt Cemetery: An Angel for its Creator

THE DOROTHEENSTADT Cemetery in Mitte is Berlin's celebrity burial ground, site of the graves of Prussian master builders Karl Friedrich Schinkel, August Stüler, Gottfried Schadow, and Christian Daniel Rauch, who created the Peace Angel on Belle-Alliance-Platz. The copper angel (opposite page) adorns Rauch's tomb. Left: The magnificent grave of Max Siegfried Borchardt, a banker and attorney general.

ALSO BURIED here are resistance fighters against the Nazis like Klaus Bonhoeffer, the brother of priest Dietrich Bonhoeffer, as well as philosophers such as G. W. F. Hegel and authors and poets like Arnold Zweig, Heinrich Mann, Anna Seghers, John Heartfield, and, most recently, Christa Wolff. Also Bert Brecht and his wife Helene Weigel are laid to rest here. Next to the cemetery was the Brecht-Keller, a restaurant where Weigel's recipes were used.

Parochial Cemetery: Cherubs in the Monastery

The Reformed Parochial Cemetery in Mitte, established in 1705, is one of the oldest preserved graveyards in Berlin. The last of the dead were buried here in 1945, civilian victims of World War II. The cemetery is associated with the Reformed Parochial Church, located next to the remains of the 700-year-old city wall. The church nave burned down during the war, along with the medieval Franciscan Grey Monastery next door, of which only the outer walls and some cherubs in the ruins remain.

Trinity, Jerusalem, and Bohemian Bethlehem

THE THREE cemeteries on Kreuzberg's main Avenue Mehringdamm were established in the 18th century, when burials were not allowed within city: the Jerusalem Cemetery, the Bethlehem Cemetery and Church (where Bohemian immigrants worshipped), and the Dreifaltigkeitsfriedhof (Trinity Cemetery), which belonged to the Dreifaltigkeitskirche, destroyed during the war. Theologist Friedrich Schleiermacher preached here in the early 19th century. Carl von Siemens, brother of inventor Werner von Siemens is buried at Trinity, guarded by the marble angel on the opposite page.

Luisenstadt Cemetery: Chalice for the Chancellor

When the cemeteries on Mehringdamm filled up, four more burial grounds were established on Kreuzberg's Bergmannstrasse, beginning in 1825: Trinity Cemetery II, Jerusalem Cemetery II, Werderscher Cemetery, and Luisenstadt Cemetery, the largest in Berlin. Many angels are standing guard. Weimar Republic Chancellor Gustav Stresemann was also laid to rest here.

Trinity Cemetery: Poets and Musicians

MANY PROMINENT Berliners are buried at Trinity and the adjacent cemeteries in Kreuzberg, such as poets E.T.A. Hoffmann and Adalbert von Chamisso, as well as master builder Georg Wenzeslaus von Knobelsdorff. Composers Felix Mendelssohn-Bartholdy and his sister, Fanny Hensel, were also laid to rest here, with their father, Abraham Mendelssohn-Bartholdy. The most beautiful white angel stands guard over the tomb of Emil Loh's family (opposite page).

Forest Cemetery: Garden of Angels

WALDFRIEDHOF ZEHLENDORF, in the southwestern district of the same name, was founded at the edge of a forest in 1946. Quite a few famous people were buried here, such as avant-garde theater director Erwin Piscator, architect Hans Scharoun, who designed the State Library at Potsdamer Strasse, architect Hermann Henselmann, who envisioned the TV tower at Alexanderplatz and Ernst Reuter, West Berlin's famed mayor. During the blockade in 1948, Reuter faced a crowd of 300,000 Berliners in front of the bombed-out Reichstag and asked the "peoples of the world not to abandon Berlin." One million mourners attended his burial. Willy Brandt was also laid to rest at Waldfriedhof, the German chancellor who began working for reconciliation with Poland in the 1970s.

The Star Who Was No Angel

"God knows, I don't want to be an angel; they live behind the sunshine, separate from us, infinitely far away. They cling to the stars so they won't fall from heaven," sang Hildegard Knef. And the singer was no angel: married three times, loved by many, especially in Berlin, where she played in 1946 in the ruins of the Schlossparktheater). After she caused a scandal by appearing nude in a movie, she left for Hollywood and Broadway. In America, she was known as Hildegard Neff. But in 2002, she was buried in the city that was her hometown, also at the Waldfriedhof. The white angel above right, next to Hilde's grave, watches over filmmaker Ulrich Schamoni.

City Angels

Ice Cream and Pie

BERLIN IS over 775 years old and is home to half a million inhabitants in many districts. Winged messengers from heaven watch over royal palaces, residences, restaurants, and snack bars alike. Some of these angels are only recognized at second glance, while others are peddled in shops and flea markets to those seeking protection. Sculptors and architects have depicted them as both happy and sad, just like the lives unfolding within the building walls, until their time has come.

The angels at right are celebrating a piece of Italy in Kreuzberg, a former ice cream parlor on Bergmannstrasse that is now a pizzeria. The angels watch over Chianti from Tuscany and Pasta Bombardoni Napoletana, as guests quench their hunger and thirst.

Pizza and Pasta: The Parliament of Angels

THERE'S ANOTHER restaurant on Bergmannstrasse that is decked out in angels—the trattoria and pizzeria *Parlamento degli Angeli* where smiling angels flutter about the walls and ceilings, holding up lamps and decorating clocks. According to owner Francesco Totti, the name of the place—A Parliament of Angels—suggests that only the best angels meet here. May all parliamentarians be angels, or at least want to be. *Buon appetito!*

Fairy Guardians of the Nikolai Quarter

In the Nikolai quarter, there's an "Angel House" that sells everything having anything to do with these winged creatures: photos, statues, winged horses (Pegasus, of course), porcelain angels, flying hearts, in gold, silver, marble, wood, carved and kitschy—it's all there. "Some angels are actually fairies," says Judith Benkhellhof, the owner of Berlin's only angel store, "You can tell by the wings." The Nikolai quarter surrounds the oldest church in the city and is a blast of refurbished past. After World War II, it was rebuilt for the city's 750-year anniversary in 1987, and is now home to many small shops and restaurants. Millions of tourists flock here, and a little angel is the ideal souvenir to tuck into a carry-on.

The Seduction of Theater Angels

BERT BRECHT wrote the poem *On the Seduction of Angels* in which he stated, "Angels are seduced either quickly or not at all." The playwright fled the Nazis to New York during World War II, then returned to post-war East Berlin. He moved his Berliner Ensemble, along with his wife, Helene Weigel, known as "Mutter Courage," into the Theater on Schiffbauerdamm. The *Threepenny Opera*, by Brecht and Kurt Weill, had premiered there in May 1928; it is a place of pilgrimage for "Brechtians." The neo-Baroque interior architecture was designed by Ernst Westphal, who included these lucky angels above the stage (left and opposite page). Above: Lotte Lenya, Weill's very own angel.

Tenements and Mansions

THE GRANDER the houses in Berlin, the more spectacular are their angels. The Jugendstil angel (right) adorns a mansion in Berlin's upscale Friedenau district. The angel frescos below watch over the City of Hamburg's embassy on Jaegerstrasse. The building was constructed in 1892 to house the *Club von Berlin* (Berlin Club), an exclusive men's club whose members included Gustav Stresemann, Richard Strauss, and Walter Gropius.

Angels of Love, Angels of Beauty

WHERE CAN the loving angels on the opposite page be found? At the Milan hair salon in Charlottenburg's Clausewitzstrasse, where we see them as God created them. Women visit hair salons to spruce up their looks, often for their loved ones. Beauty and love go hand in hand, after all. How did the poet Heinrich Heine put it? "The angels call it Heaven's delight. The devils call it Hades' fright. But men just call it love!" And there are all kinds of angels at Berlin flea markets and antique stores, like those found in Tiergarten's Turmstrasse, a street known for its thrift stores; here and on the previous page.

Wall Angels—Art along the Spree

The East Side Gallery is an open-air art show of a special kind: After the peaceful revolution in the GDR, when the Wall fell in November 1989, artists came from many countries to East Berlin to paint a one-mile stretch of the Wall on the east side of the Spree River. They wanted to commemorate those who brought down the Wall and the Cold War with it. But the Gallery was also an expression of joy at their new-found freedom. Artists Karina Bjerregaard and Lotte Haubert painted wings on their figures, because from 1961 to 1989, Berliners actually would have needed wings to get over the Wall. Their painting is reminiscent of the landmark film by Wim Wenders, *Wings of Desire*.

Christmas Angels

Festive Gendarmenmarkt

During the weeks before Christmas, almost one hundred Christmas markets open in Berlin, in a variety of sizes, with hot mulled wine, bratwurst, carousels, and hundreds of gifts, from marzipan to Christmas tree ornaments, to the sounds of Christmas carols and pop music. Here at the Gendarmenmarkt, the most contemplative Christmas market in town, between the German and French Cathedrals, this golden angel of glory watches over his gingerbread realm. The gingerbread is from an organic farm near Würzburg named *New Jerusalem*. Unlike the rest of the sweet things all around him, this one's not for sale, because this lovely boy with the curly hair is just a decoration.

Carousel Angels on Alexanderplatz

The Christmas market on Alexanderplatz is a little less contemplative, but it's a tradition that continued through the GDR era, when it was a favorite destination for West Berliners, too. These angels decorate carnival rides and carousels that lure visitors—especially children—out of the surrounding stores.

Angels of Memories, Angels of Remembrance

THIS ANGEL (right) greets us from the entrance to the Kaiser Wilhelm Memorial Church between the Zoo and Kurfürstendamm, the Western part of Berlin. Mosaics by Hermann Schaper decorate the entryway, representations of the life of Kaiser Wilhelm I. The 1895 church was destroyed on February 23, 1943. The ruin today is a place of remembrance and contemplation of the wounds of war, but also of peace and forgiveness. A new church was built next to the ruin, a slender tower designed by Egon Eiermann. The little angels on the left adorn the Christmas Market in front of the church. And the angel above, playing the trumpet used to be weather vane on the Berlin Cathedral in the East. Today, angels from the East and West are united once again!

Berlinica presents

New books 2023-2025

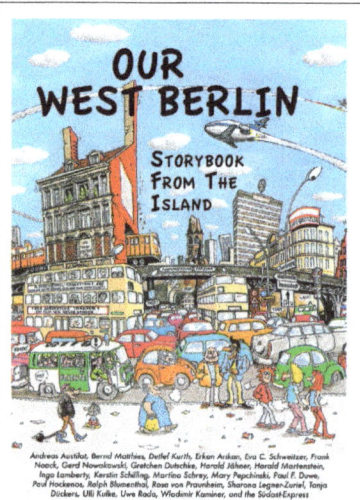

Softcover, bw, 80 pics; $22.95
Dimensions: 240 pp; 6 x 9"
ISBN: 978-1-935902-54-6
        978-3-96026-067-7

Softcover, full color, 66 pics; $18.00
Dimensions: 100 pp; 6 x 9"
ISBN: 978-3-96026-080-6
        978-3-96026-089-9

Softcover, bw, 67 pics; $14.00
Dimensions: 176 pp; 5.5 x 8.5"
ISBN: 978-3-96026-069-1
Hardcover is forthcoming

Softcover, bw, 12 pics; $16.00
Dimensions: 176 pp; 5.5 x 8.5"
ISBN: 978-3-96026-066-0
        978-3-96026-064-6

Softcover, color, 44 pics; $18.00
Dimensions: 170 pp; 5.5 x 8.5"
ISBN: 978-3-96026-073-8
        HC: 978-1-935902-73-7

Softcover, color, 165 pics; $22.95
Dimensions: 224 pp; 6 x 9"
ISBN: 978-1-935902-55-3
Hardcover: 978-1-935902-58-4

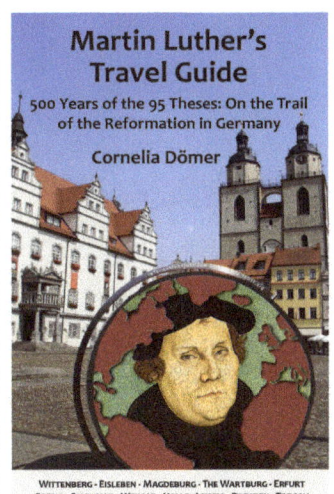

Softcover/French flaps, full color
140 pics and maps; $14.00
Dimensions: 176 pp; 5 x 8"
ISBN: 978-1-935902-44-7

Hardcover, bw, 12 pics; $20.00
Dimensions: 208 pp; 6 x 9"
ISBN: 978-1-935902-65-2
          978-3-96026-016-5

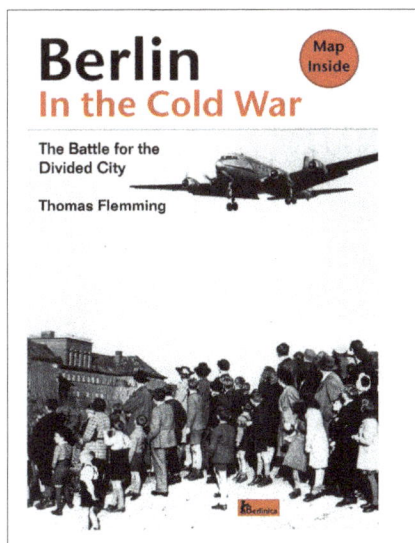

Softcover, s/w, 51 pics; $12.99
Dimensions: 90 pp; 7' x 10"
ISBN: 978-3-96026-006-6
          978-3-96026-090-5

Softcover, color, 117 pics; $16.95
Dimensions: 102 pp; 8.5 x 8.5"
ISBN: 978-1-935902-10-2
          978-3-96026-079-0

Softcover, bw, 177 pics; $24.95
Dimensions: 218 pp; 8.5 x11.0"
ISBN: 978-3-96026-014-1
          978-3-96026-002-8

Softcover, bw, 25 pics; $14.95
Dimensions: 202 pp; 5.5 x 8.5"
ISBN: 978-1-935902-20-1
       978-3-96026-027-1

Hardcover, sepia, 23 pics; $14.95
Dimensions: 96 pp; 5 x 8"
ISBN: 978-1-935902-89-8
       978-3-96026-028-8

Softcover, bw, 8 pics; $14.95
Dimensions: 208 pp; 5.5 x 8.5"
ISBN: 978-3-96026-025-7
       978-3-96026-086-8

Hardcover, color, 18 pics; $14.95
Dimensions: 96 pp; 5 x 8"
ISBN: 978-1-935902-25-6
       978-1-935902-27-0

Softcover, sw, 21 pics; $20.00
Dimensions: 256 pp; 6 x 9"
ISBN: 978-3-96026-015-8
       978-3-96026-098-1

Softcover, bw, 2 pics; $13.95
Dimensions: 144 pp; 5 x 8"
ISBN: 978-3-96026-071-4
       978-3-96026-042-4

www.ingramcontent.com/pod-product-compliance
Lightning Source LLC
LaVergne TN
LVHW071547050725
815454LV00020B/371